Foot

F
BEST FOOT FORWARD

O
Kathy

01

Vanderlinden

A PLAYFUL   BIOGRAPHY

MAINSTREAM
PUBLISHING

EDINBURGH AND LONDON

First published in the Canada in 2003 by
Greystone Books
A Division of Douglas & McIntyre Ltd.

First published in Great Britain in 2003 by
MAINSTREAM PUBLISHING (EDINBURGH) LTD
7 Albany Street
Edinburgh EH1 3UG

ISBN 1 84018 798 0

A catalogue record for this book is available from the British Library

Designed by Peter Cocking & Jessica Sullivan
Typeset in Garamond No. 3, among others

Printed and bound in China by C.S. Graphics Pte. Ltd.

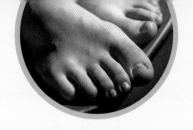

· · · · · ·

$\mathcal{S}$how me a **man**

WITH BOTH **FEET** ON THE GROUND

and $\mathcal{I}$'ll **show** you

A MAN WHO

can't put his **pants** on.

ARTHUR K. WATSON

· · · · · ·

STEPPING

$\mathcal{F}$**EET AROUSE** contradictory responses. Some people rhapsodize about them; others consider them a regrettable design flaw best concealed by aesthetically corrective footwear.

Feet resonate on both ends of the pain–pleasure scale, too. On the one hand (or foot), they are notoriously prone to a host of afflictions, from corns to plantar fasciitis; on the other, feet can deliver delicious sensations and are highly favored by fetishists.

FOOT [FOOT] *N., PL.*

FEET. THE LOWER END OF

THE LEG FROM

THE ANKLE THROUGH

THE TOES.

OUT

Above all, the foot is a symbolic shape-shifter, literally the most down-to-earth thing we've got and also one of the most allusive. When deep in our evolutionary past we chose to walk on two feet, we shifted more onto them than the full weight of our bodies; we also added a potential load of metaphorical baggage.

Our feet are our contact with the earth—they literally ground us. To prehistoric minds, that earthiness linked them to the material realm and made them a conduit for evil spirits. Since then, we have judged the earthy foot variously as impure, base, humble, innocent, or—most definitely—sexy. After all, our upright stance made us permanent flashers, exposing our erogenous zones and creating a uniquely human sexuality. Feet came to symbolize sex and all our ambivalent feelings about it.

With all this going on, it's no wonder we have a pedal fixation, and it starts early. At birth, the first question after "Boy or girl?" is, "Does it have all its fingers and toes?" Adults are irresistibly drawn to babies' tiny feet, holding them, kissing them, and playing "This little piggy" games. Babies themselves soon discover the sensuous pleasure of their feet and instinctively put them where the action is—in their mouths. It's the beginning of a beautiful, complex relationship.

Do the Locomotion

. . . .

*E*VOLUTIONALLY SPEAKING, walking on two feet is a very big deal. In a basic sense, it's our most human characteristic. As far as we know, it all started at least 4 million years ago, when some hominids—a group of apelike species that preceded us—started walking upright. It was the first clearly human thing they did after branching off from the rest of the apes,

If the shoe fits, X-ray it

. . . .

From the 1920s to '50s, shoe stores across North America and Europe displayed magical box-like devices called shoe-fitting fluoroscopes that showed customers X-ray pictures of their feet. The four- or five-foot-tall box housed an X-ray tube with a lead-lined base and a fluorescent screen on which images were projected. Shoppers would insert their newly shod feet into an opening near the bottom of the box and peer down through a port on top. At the flick of a switch, they could marvel at the sight of their toes wriggling inside perfectly fitted footwear. Oblivious to danger, shoe buyers thought nothing of irradiating themselves and to some extent everyone else nearby. Worse, many devices were faulty, emitting even more radiation than expected. But eventually public awareness caught up with commerce, and by the late '50s, shoe-fitting fluoroscopes were widely banned and soon disappeared from the cultural stage.

. . . .

and scientists have long been interested in establishing when they did it, a date that keeps getting shifted backward as new discoveries are made. Fossil-bone fragments found in Africa have shown adaptations for bipedal walking, such as reorganization of the hip and knee joints. But the most evocative find was likely a 75-foot trail of footprints excavated in Tanzania around 1976.

The trail indicated that at least two hominids had walked there slowly, side by side, close enough to be touching, about 3.6 million years ago. The area was crisscrossed with the prints of other animals, too—elephants, rhinos, saber-toothed cats—but these were different. They looked startlingly human, with straight-facing big toes and a human-like gait pattern, and they ➤

All my fortunes at thy foot I'll lay,

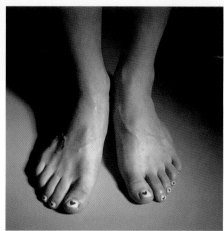

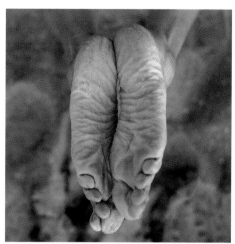

And follow thee my lord throughout the world.

WILLIAM SHAKESPEARE, ROMEO AND JULIET

were made by individuals about 4′9″ and 4′1″ tall—possibly a male and female. The smaller one may have been carrying something, perhaps a baby, a suggestion that conjures up the irresistible, though perhaps fanciful, image of a vastly distant ancestral family out for a stroll.

When archaeologists placed these bipedal walkers in history, they had to push back estimates of upright walking a million years. Since then, new finds have moved the date back even further, to 4.2 or possibly 5 million years ago.

Cinderella Complex

. . . .

*A*SENTIMENTAL CHILDREN'S TALE about a poor, virtuous girl marrying up and living happily ever after? Not exactly. The aptly named Brothers Grimm were poles from Disney when in the 1880s they penned their version of "Cinderella" (or "Aschenputtel"). In their telling, Stepmom cut off her first and second daughters' big toe and heel, respectively, in a non-maternal attempt to snatch a prince for a son-in-law. Only the blood on their white wedding stockings (crash of symbols there) foiled her plan and paved the way for the youngest daughter, the one with the tiniest feet. Nor does Cinderella forgive her sisters, who will now have a hard time finding shoes, let alone husbands, as a result of Mom's folly. In the end, birds pluck out their eyes.

Not that the Grimms invented these chilling details. The Cinderella story, one of the most popular folktales of all time, exists in hundreds of versions (some with male Cinderfellas) based on oral traditions dating back at least to 9th-century China and, in the slipper element, to ancient Egypt some 5,000 years ago. The familiar pretty features—fairy godmother, pumpkin coach, rat footmen, and Cinderella's forgiving gesture—were introduced in 1697 by the French author Charles Perrault, whose refinements found their way into many contemporary versions. In more recent centuries, this archetypal tale has been the subject of intense scrutiny by folklorists and psychologists such as Bruno Bettel-heim, who saw in the Grimm telling a dark tangle of sibling rivalry, oedipal complexes, and castration sym-bols that helped kids deal with their unconscious fears.

With so many interpreta-tions of the tale already on offer, here's another. In a mod-ern reading, the true victims might be seen as those wicked stepsisters. Was their real crime a failure to be "little women"?

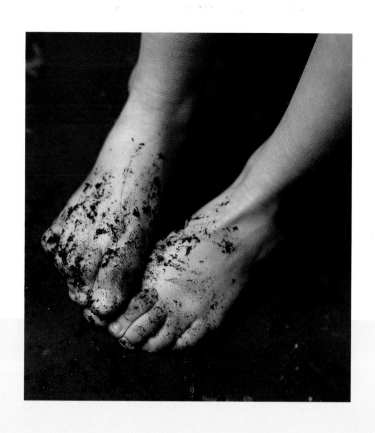

*Forget not that the
earth **delights** to feel your bare
feet and the winds
long to play with your hair.*

KAHLIL GIBRAN

You Sexy Feet

LOSE-UP ON A YOUNG female foot. A man's left hand reaches under to cradle it, while his right hand gently pushes a cotton tuft between the first two toes, then brushes polish on the first nail. His hands move tenderly from toe to toe, insinuating the cotton and then applying the paint. As he works, the toes arch in response. Over this exquisitely erotic scene the credits roll for *Lolita*, Stanley Kubrick's 1962 film based on Vladimir Nabokov's story of abject, transgressive love.

Oh yes, feet are sexy, and for several good reasons. First, they are expressive touch organs, their skin packed with nerves responsive to light touch, as well as nerves specific to erogenous zones such as the palms, lips, eyelids, external genitals, and nipples. Further, the structure of the feet offers delicate curves, hollows, protuberances, and scents that can suggest genitals or breasts. Stroking, kissing, licking, or sucking on the toes or inner arch can send lovers into raptures.

Healthy feet are aesthetic masterpieces, too, their beauty recognized by many painters and sculptors. Notice the fleshy luminance of skin tones, the spread of the toes and curve of an arch, the glimpse of sole, the fluid, expressive gestures. Even

OUCH!

Most women—one study by the American Orthopedic Foot and Ankle Society found 90 percent— wear shoes that are too small for them. Not surprisingly, those same tight shoes cause 90 percent of women's foot deformities. Women are nine times more likely than men to suffer foot problems caused by ill-fitting shoes.

the rather ordinary foot of the nude girl in Manet's *Déjeuner sur l'herbe* carries a sexual charge, with its challenging nakedness and the upward arc of that big toe.

Women (and a few men) use their feet to telegraph sexuality, usually through footwear. The swooping top of the foot (intensi- fied in high heels), the fine-boned ankle, and the toe cleavage are displayed to advantage by sandals and low-cut vamps. Straps and buckles suggest bondage, and narrow pointed toes signal submis- siveness, especially if the stance is toed in. Shoes and boots that cover up the feet can scream "I'm sexy!" too, by constricting the foot with leather and lacings. (Old symbols die hard.)

Feet are supremely sexy too, no doubt, just because they are laden with taboos. Dirt, humility, earthiness, degradation— oh, baby!

I HAVE SPREAD

MY *dreams*

UNDER YOUR FEET;

tread SOFTLY

BECAUSE YOU TREAD ON *my dreams.*

W.B. YEATS, HE WISHES FOR THE CLOTHS OF HEAVEN

Oh, Manolo!

. . . .

MANY WOMEN LOVE SHOES, but they love some shoes much, much more than others. Manolo Blahniks, for example. The Spanish-born designer's creations are a kind of Holy Grail of shoes, revered by rich, stylish, and rapturous collectors everywhere. Blahnik hand-sews very expensive shoes (often costing thousands of dollars) of exquisite sexiness, beauty, luxury, and often whimsy, many of which find their way onto the feet of luminaries such as Isabella Rossellini, Paloma Picasso, Madonna, Kate Moss, and Sarah Jessica Parker, as well as legions of less stellar Manolo collectors. Many of his fans are frankly unhinged about both the footgear and the guy himself and

storm the shops bearing armloads of shoes for him to autograph whenever he makes an appearance.

And Blahnik earns the adulation. A consummate showman—flamboyant, temperamental, eccentric—he owns a weekend house in Bath whose four stories and attic are crammed wall to wall and ceiling to floor with examples of his art. As befits a star, he's

Anatomy of a Foot

The foot is a physiological marvel, with 26 bones—7 tarsal bones in the heel and instep, 5 metatarsals in the ball of the foot, and 14 phalanges making up the toes. Together, the feet account for one-quarter of all the bones in the human body. The arch allows us to walk upright by absorbing punishing shocks and supporting the body's weight. Each foot also contains 33 joints, 107 ligaments, 19 muscles, and a complex network of blood vessels and nerves.

The feet are packed with nerve endings—more than 7,000 in each one (see "You Sexy Feet"). Their rich innervation makes them supersensitive to touch, pressure, pain, heat, and cold, even though the skin of the sole is the thickest in the body—about one-eighth of an inch. Nerve impulses from the feet are processed in the sensory parietal lobe of the neocortex, occupying more space in the brain "map" than does the entire torso.

contradictory—he's a clean freak, but he likes the idea of his shoes being worn in the mud. Even as a child growing up in the Canary Islands he was an original, fashioning tiny shoes of tinfoil, ribbon, and lace for lizards, birds, dogs, and cats. Blahnik was inspired by his stylish mother, who made her own clogs and espadrilles because she wasn't happy with those available locally.

Blahnik designs all his own shoes, has them made by hand, and would personally cut and sew them all if he had time. Crafted from exotic skins and sumptuous fabrics trimmed with feathers, sequins, fur, and jewels, and typically equipped with vertiginous heels, his shoes often walk the edge of the possible. In fact, a design for his 2002 spring show did go that little step further. ➤

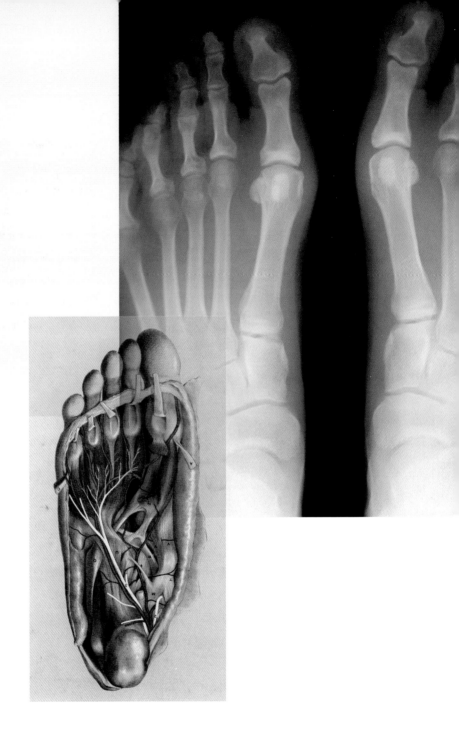

What spirit is so empty and blind, that it cannot recognize the fact
that the foot is more noble than the shoe, and skin more beautiful
than the garment with which it is clothed?

MICHELANGELO

Tennis, anyone?

Jacek Guzowski of Poland juggled a tennis ball with his feet for a record-breaking 5 hours, 28 minutes, 59 seconds on November 11, 1999. His feet touched the ball an average of 1.8 times per second.

The three-and-a-half-inch titanium heel of the 500-dollar stiletto was as thin as a ballpoint pen cartridge and would skewer floors, carpets, and any foot unlucky enough to get under it. Blahnik eventually withdrew the shoe, not because it was impossible to walk in (women can learn to leap tall buildings in any fashionable footgear) but to prevent customer injuries, lawsuits, and run-ins with airport security personnel.

Once Upon a Foot

*I*T SEEMS THAT FEET are the reason we have a Mother Goose and not, say, a Mother Bear. The most popular theory is that they belonged to a real queen, an 8th-century French royal named Berthe, the wife of Pépin le Bref and mother of the famous Charlemagne. Her most notable attribute was an uncommonly large foot. Whether it was a clubfoot or the result of too much foot-pedaling (the queen was an expert spinner), her affliction earned poor Berthe the nickname "the goose-footed queen," and church statues said to be modeled on her bear that inscription.

The spinning element also connects Berthe to Mother Goose, since in medieval Europe, flax-spinning halls were popular sites for telling folktales, a raucous way to ease the tedium of the work. The risk of developing a monster appendage was apparently a hazard of the job. In old France, the phrase "Au temps que la reine Berthe filait" (When Queen Berthe was spinning) was a popular way to begin a tale, much like "Once upon a time."

The story would end there, except that there was another French Queen Berthe, who lived in the 11th century and who was also a spinner and had goose associations. This Berthe caused a scandal by marrying a close relative, Robert II. Threatened with excommunication, Robert divorced Berthe in 1023, but not before they had produced a son with the head and neck of a goose. This Berthe may therefore be the real "goose-footed queen." It's also possible that both Berthes were perfectly normal and that the goose details were grafted on from Teutonic swan-maiden myths.

In any case, in the 17th century, books of fairy tales for children appeared portraying "la mère l'oye" as a craggy peasant woman surrounded by a group of rapt children, often with a spinning wheel nearby. Gradually, most remnants of Queen Berthe were submerged in a soft-featured, non-spinning granny with regular feet, or a cartoon goose wearing a big bonnet.

By'r lady, your **LADYSHIP** *is nearer*

to **HEAVEN** *than when I saw you last,*

by the altitude of a **CHOPINE**.

WILLIAM SHAKESPEARE, HAMLET

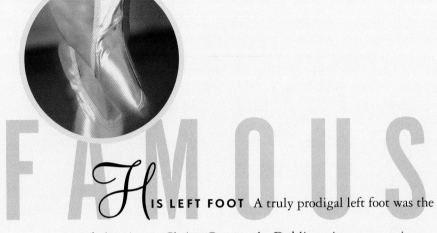

FAMOUS

*H*IS LEFT FOOT A truly prodigal left foot was the one belonging to Christy Brown, the Dublin writer, poet, painter, and subject of the memorable 1989 movie *My Left Foot.* Born in 1932 with cerebral palsy, Brown had no control over any part of his body except that one foot, but it was enough to link him to the outer world. Everyone but his mother had assumed he was severely mentally disabled until the day, when he was five, that he grabbed

DANCE [DANS] *VB*.

· · · · · ·

MOVE ABOUT

· · · · · ·

RHYTHMICALLY, USUALLY

· · · · · ·

TO MUSIC.

FEET

a piece of chalk with his left foot and made a mark on the floor.

That was the beginning of an extraordinary life, though not a

saintly one. Brown was courageous, brilliant, witty, as well as

manipulative, rude-mouthed, and a boozer. Ironically, his story

may be more commonly associated with the dishily footed Daniel

Day-Lewis, who won a Best Actor Oscar for his portrayal of

Brown in the movie.

Dorothy's Shoes

The most famous shoes in the history of film, if not the Western world, are probably the ruby slippers Judy Garland wore in the 1939 movie *The Wizard of Oz*. The magic schoolgirl pumps in which Dorothy skipped down the yellow brick road have become cult items revered by *Oz* fans and collectors of film memorabilia. Covered in red silk studded with sequins, bugle beads, and rhinestones, the shoes departed from the silver slippers of the original L. Frank Baum story to take advantage of Technicolor.

The thing is, this unique pair of movie shoes is not in fact unique. At least four and maybe seven pairs of *Oz* slippers are known to exist and more may be out there somewhere. As is standard practice for important costumes, MGM's wardrobe department had several copies made. One pair is now in the Smithsonian Institution, another travels around to various exhibits, and at least two others are in private collections. One of these was bought in 2000 by a California collector for a whopping U.S. $666,000.

REALLY, SIR RALEIGH? The feet of Queen Elizabeth I are famous not for themselves but for their role as cultural symbol. When Sir Walter Raleigh spread his cape over a puddle to protect the queenly feet, he created our consummate image of gallantry. Never mind that it probably didn't happen. As captain of the queen's guard, he had lain at her feet metaphorically for years. Muddying his cape for her would have been small potatoes.

SEXTET Did Marilyn Monroe have six toes on each foot? Rather disappointingly, no. It seems this popular urban myth is based on two photos taken in 1946, when Marilyn was still Norma Jean and her feet were unlegendary. The photographer, Joseph Jasgur, didn't notice anything odd about the shots until some 40 years later, when he decided to publish them in a book. One shot is too fuzzy to make out, but the other could fool a person. It is a worm's-eye view of Marilyn's left foot, which appears to have six digits. On closer inspection, though, the sixth "toe" is likely a foreshortened view of the outer curve of the instep. Other pictures of the foot taken around the same time clearly show five digits. Like the rest of her, Marilyn's toes were perfectly okay.

FOOT VÉRITÉ In movies, the actors' shoes can help suspend disbelief or cause it to plummet. Samuele Mazza in *Cinderella's Revenge* writes that the Italian film director Luchino Visconti insisted that even the most minor actors in his movies wear shoes of the correct style and period; otherwise, their modern walk would give them away. Federico Fellini was another purist. For his 1976 film *Casanova,* he made the actors wear perfect copies of 18th-century shoes, which are brutal on contemporary feet and caused the actors no end of misery. Apparently the shoes are still in excellent condition because no one will steal them or rent them for other films.

MOONWALKERS The first earthling foot to touch the moon (or any celestial body) belonged to the U.S. astronaut Neil Armstrong, commander of the *Apollo 11* lunar voyage. He made the ➤

MAN IS A *wingless animal* WITH TWO **FEET** *and flat nails.*

PLATO

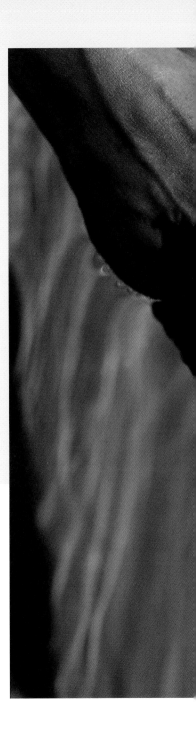

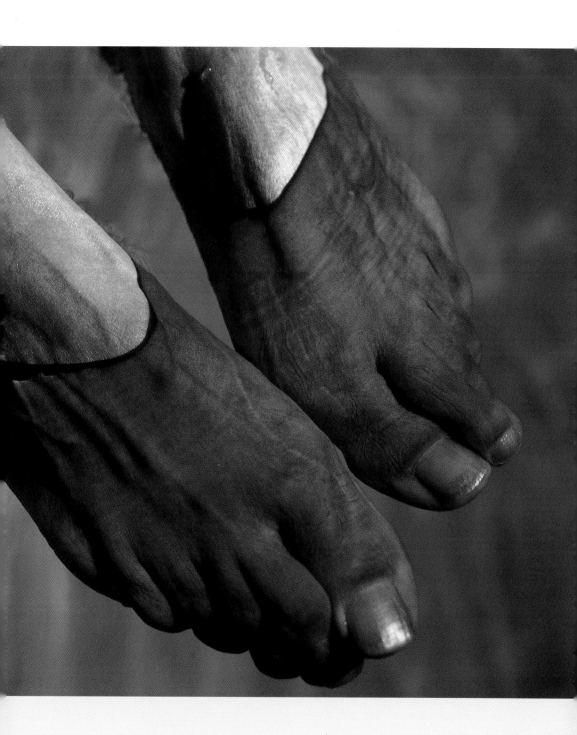

. . . .

Falling asleep depends on your feet. Researchers have found that in late evening, the blood vessels in your feet and hands automatically dilate, warming them in preparation for sleep—the warmer they are, the faster you nod off.

historic contact on July 20, 1969. Shortly after stepping down onto the moon's powdery surface, Armstrong broadcast his "one small step for [a] man, one giant leap for mankind" speech to the awestruck inhabitants of planet Earth, now glowing "pretty and blue" in the heavens above him.

HOW MANY, REALLY? Imelda Marcos, former First Lady of the Philippines, has become the popular symbol of wanton shoe excess. But how many pairs did she actually have? When she and her husband fled the country, news sources reported that she'd owned a stack of 3,000; others estimated 1,200 pairs. She herself has admitted to only 1,060.

BIGFOOT The world's most famous semi-human feet undoubtedly belong to Bigfoot (a.k.a. the Sasquatch, Abominable Snowman, Mapinguari, Yowie, and Yeti), a prehistoric apelike biped reputed to be 7 to 10 feet tall with feet some 17 inches long. But does Bigfoot really exist? Yes, Virginia, as long as there are aliens from outer space, werewolves, succubi, and other creatures that go bump in the middle of our collective unconscious. But perhaps that is too skeptical a view. To be fair, it's a tug of war. You have the scientists, who tend to be spoilsports, and you have the enthusiasts, who believe. Indeed, there have been countless sightings in many parts of the world—in China going back some 2,300 years, and in North America gathering steam since the 19th century. Besides the sightings, the evidence consists of a few blurry films and several footprint casts (many clearly faked but others not so easily dismissed).

FOOTSIE FOLLY Sarah, Duchess of York must be on any list of famous feet by virtue of the infamous toe-sucking escapade of 1992. That summer, the whole world was titillated by tabloid photos of Fergie lounging poolside in the south of France, while her Texas business advisor, John Bryan, nibbled on her toes. The Queen, however—not to mention Prince Andrew—was not amused.

Amelia's Sole?

The disappearance of Amelia Earhart in 1937 during an around-the-world flight attempt immediately spawned a string of exotic rumors. She'd been a government spy, sent to check out suspected Japanese military installations. She'd been interned in a prison camp. She was perfectly well and living in America. The official explanation was that her plane had plunged into the sea. Apparently the true story lies somewhere in between, and a key clue is a shoe—or rather, a Cat's Paw heel, four bits of rubber sole, and a brass shoelace eyelet, found in 1991 on the tiny mid-Pacific island of Nikumaroro. Evidence gathered over the years suggests that Earhart and Fred Noonan, her navigator, made an emergency landing there. The sole was manufactured in the mid-1930s and belonged to a woman's size 8 ½ or 9 blucher-style oxford, the type of shoe Earhart was wearing in a photograph taken 10 days before she vanished.

Nay,
her **FOOT** speaks;

her wanton spirits look out

At every joint and motive

of her body.

WILLIAM SHAKESPEARE, TROILUS AND CRESSIDA

39

The Ornamented Foot

. . . .

*T*HE NATURAL BEAUTY and sensuality of the foot invite decoration—toe rings, anklets, paints, and tattoos. One of the oldest and gentlest forms of foot adornment is henna painting, which goes back 5,000 years to Egypt, where henna was a kind of all-purpose cosmetic, medicine, skin conditioner, and good-luck charm. Mummies have been uncovered with feet, hands, hair, and shroud still tinted with the maroon-red dye. Henna painting spread throughout the East and is still popular in many countries. In India, where it is known as *mehndi,* it is an integral and joyous part of the Hindu wedding ceremony.

The night before the wedding, the bride and her female relatives and friends gather for the *mehndi* party, a combination rite of passage, sacred ceremony, and giddy celebration. The bride's (and maybe the groom's) feet, hands, and sometimes other parts of the body are painted with delicate paisley, floral, or geometric designs that can symbolize fertility, eternity, or the cycle of life. These patterns covering the top of the foot, lacing between toes, and trailing up the shin act as a spiritual shield (especially important at times of transition) and a prayer for the couple's happiness, good fortune, and lasting love.

To make the paint, crushed henna leaf is mixed with black tea, a fragrant oil, and perhaps some lemon juice. The designs are drawn on with an applicator and a steady hand, then dabbed with lemon juice and sugar, and left to set for several hours to create the darkest line possible. The bride understands that the darker it is, the luckier she is, and the more the groom loves her.

Since the '90s, body art of all kinds has taken off in North America. Supermodels use henna designs as temporary or trial tattoos, and more and more, a real tattoo is the decoration of choice for those ready to make a lifetime commitment to patterned feet—oh, and to put up with a little pain. The process has improved since its back-street days. State-of-the-art tattooing, which uses electric machinery and scrupulous sanitation practices, is easier, safer, and better tolerated than, say, having the needles pounded in with a little hammer (another technique).

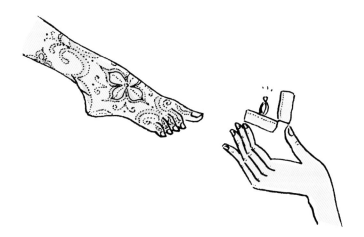

Why

ISN'T THERE A

special name

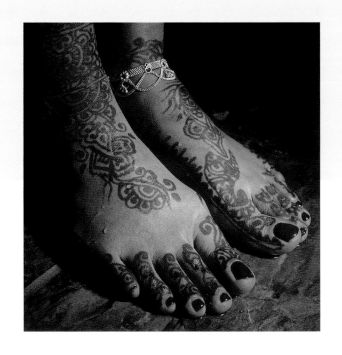

FOR THE *tops*

OF YOUR FEET?

LILY TOMLIN

The Measuring Foot

. . . .

*J*T OCCURRED TO PEOPLE early on that the foot made a convenient measuring tool, and almost all cultures since the
ancient Egyptians have used it. Since human feet come in
different lengths, rough standards had to be set. The "natural foot"
(pes naturalis) was an early unit of about 9.8 inches (25 centimeters), but it was soon replaced in Middle Eastern cultures by a
longer foot that fit proportionally with other established natural
units—for example, palms (widths) and digits (finger widths).
This foot equaled 4 palms or 16 digits.

As civilizations progressed, each culture adopted its own
"foot," which could vary even from city to city. There were
at least two Greek feet as well as a Roman foot, and
the northern Europeans had the "manual foot" *(pes
manualis)*, which was based on the hand—the
length of two hands grasping a rod with
thumbs outstretched and touching.

A modern foot of about 12 inches
(30.5 centimeters), possibly an innova-
tion of Henry I, appeared after the
Norman conquest of 1066, but until
the 14th century, a "foot" might be
the actual foot-length of whatever

FOOTWORK

. . . .

Each day, the average person
takes 8,000 to 10,000 steps, in the
process exerting a force on the feet
equal to several hundred tons. Over a
lifetime, the same average person
walks some 115,000 miles, which is like
hiking all the way around the earth
more than four times. Women are
super-walkers, averaging one-third
more walking distance than men,
often in high heels.

monarch was on the throne at the time. Eventually most of the world's nations agreed to the international foot, established as exactly 30.48 centimeters in the Weights and Measures Act of 1963. But an older infinitesimally larger foot, called the "survey foot," is still used in the United States for geodetic surveying, and the practice of pacing off an area will never die.

Is That a Shoe in Your Pocket...?

· ·

*T*HE SEXUAL FETISH came to public attention probably as a result of Richard von Krafft-Ebing's 1886 study *Psychopathia Sexualis,* which described the fetishes of hundreds of his most deviant patients, the majority of whom were obsessed with feet. Intended for doctors, the book was a hit with general readers, who probably wanted to know whether other people took shoes to bed, or it was just them.

Although a fetish can be almost anything (a shine on the nose was one of Freud's wilder examples), foot and shoe fetishes are by far the most common. According to one estimate, about one in 200 men have a special regard for feet or footwear. Foot fetishism is thought to be very much a male preserve, although it's not clear why. Women may just be more likely—and able, since perform-ance is not at issue—to hide what society considers perverse. ➤

It's the most wonderful *feel.*

The grass is so soft.

The **daisies** *tickle*

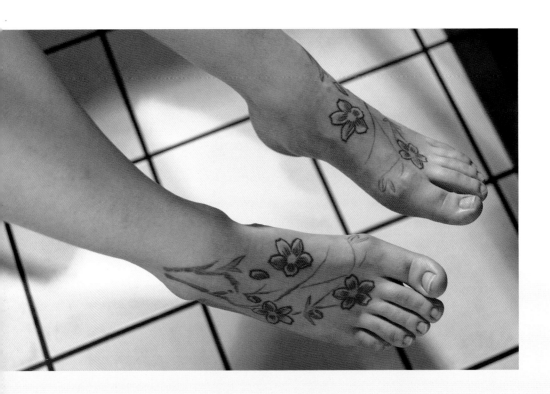

and leave pink *and* white *petals*

on your **naked** *feet.*

EMILY CARR, HUNDREDS AND THOUSANDS

Fetish web sites suggest that women are beginning to emerge from the closet, some with shoes in hand. (But no, having a thing for shoes and shoe shopping is not considered a fetish, or the the whole category would crumble.)

Of course, feet are widely acknowledged to be erogenous zones (see "You Sexy Feet"), and you don't have to be Freud to see how feet and shoes might symbolize male and female genitalia respectively. (Although, since symbolism is notoriously fluid, shoes can be phallic, too. Consider the pointed toe or the stiletto—except when it

gets caught in a grate, and then a heel is just a heel.) What makes foot appreciation a fetish is a matter of degree. The fetishist is aroused exclusively by feet.

A fetish can range from mild (always wanting your partner to wear boots during sex) to extreme (stealing the boots off strangers' feet to add to your collection of 300 pairs, which is your sole source of sexual fulfillment). Most fetishes revolve around certain themes and narratives—erotic scenarios played out in imagination or acted out repeatedly. A shoe fetishist (a.k.a. bootman) might act out a fantasy of polishing the shoes of a haughty woman or being stomped on by a pair of high heels. For some fetishists, transgression itself is a turn-on, and in extreme cases the fetish can veer into dangerous and violent territory.

Ticklish Matters

Feet are exquisitely ticklish—next to the armpits and ribs, they're the most ticklish parts of the body. Many people find foot tickling a source of intense erotic pleasure.

Throughout history, royals and aristocrats have been particularly fond of foot tickling. The great Egyptian female pharaoh Hatshepsut (who reigned 1503–1482 BCE) is said to have prepared for lovers by having the palace eunuchs massage her feet with scented oils, then tickle the soles with peacock feathers. Catherine the Great and other members of the Russian nobility were also addicted. Sometimes a czarina would have her feet tickled to the accompaniment of lewd songs or stories, to bring her passion to fever pitch.

Foot fetishes may have their roots in early childhood. Some begin with specific experiences that form associations between feet and pleasure. A sexually repressive background can also be a catalyst, making regular sex so fearful to a child that his erotic impulses shift to the safer region of the leg and foot. Neurological factors may also play a part.

But whether the fetish is a problem for the fetishist depends on the individual. Those at the extreme end may seek treatment in the form of cognitive therapy and drugs that dampen the libido. Others see no need to put the boot to a practice they so richly enjoy. After all, they are in good company. Charles Baudelaire, Thomas Hardy, and F. Scott Fitzgerald are reputed foot fetishists; Omar Kayyam, Leo Tolstoy, and Fyodor Dostoevsky were rumored to be bootmen.

An' I seed her first a-smokin'
of a whackin' white cheroot,
An' a-wastin' Christian kisses
on an 'eathen idol's foot.

RUDYARD KIPLING, MANDALAY

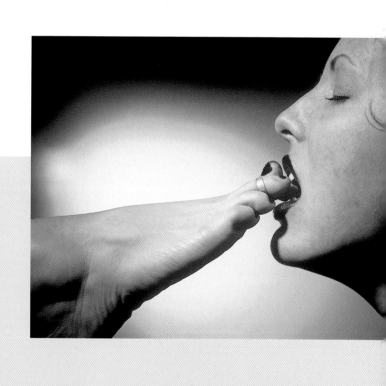

FOLIES À

The foot is basically a wedge, but shoe-makers don't want to know. Consider but two examples from history: the chopine and the poulaine.

Today's high heels and platforms are almost wimpy compared to the contraptions worn by Venetian courtesans and wealthy trendsetters of the Renaissance. With a platform sole averaging 6 to 18 inches, the chopine defined the height of fashion literally.

LEAP [LĒP] *VB.*

. . . . . .

SPRING INTO

. . . . . .

THE AIR.

DEUX

The tallest versions were as high as stilts, and wearers needed

servants to help them navigate the roughly paved streets without

breaking their necks. The desire to be stylish was so compelling

that a Venetian law in 1430 banning the chopine (to prevent

an imagined rash of miscarriages and monstrous births)

was regularly ignored. The style was popular off and on for

200 years and spread throughout Europe.

An earlier extravaganza, the poulaine, which was popular in Europe in the 14th and 15th centuries, explored the far reaches of fashion horizontally. The most extreme version, also known as a pike or cracow (after the Polish centre), was a flat shoe with a long pointed toe often stuffed with wool, hair, or moss to keep it straight or slightly up-curved. The tip was useful for under-the-table dalliance. Legend has it that some toe points were so long they had to be attached to the knee or even the waist with laces or chains. Government and clergy felt compelled to intervene and set length limits, but moral censure did little to dampen people's enthusiasm. Echoes of pike passion still show up from time to time, notably in the British winkle-picker of the 1960s.

The Magnificent Seven

. . . .

THE VARIETY OF GEAR you can put on your feet seems infinite, but according to one theory, all of it can be shoe-horned into some combination of just seven basic styles.

MOCCASIN Our first shoe idea was a piece of animal skin gathered and tied around the ankle with a rawhide thong. That 14,000-year-old protector developed into the moccasin, from an Algonquian word meaning "foot covering." Essentially a one- or two-piece hide shoe with a soft sole, the moccasin was worn by many northern peoples and probably originated with Mongol tribes, who then brought it to North America. Aboriginal groups added beads, fringes, and other decorations in patterns that could signify the wearer's rank or occupation.

SANDAL The sandal dates back at least 10,000 years. Its name probably comes from an ancient Persian word for sandal, *sanis,* meaning "slab" or "board." Ancient sandals indicated a person's status, not only by style (there have always been hundreds of designs) but by virtue of being worn at all. High-ranking Egyptians, for instance, wore sandals of woven palm fibers or tanned hides, the latter being most prestigious; elite women encrusted theirs with jewels, and slaves and poor people went barefoot. And in 200 CE, the Roman emperor Aurelius decreed that only he and his successors could wear red sandals. But around 1000, sandals took a very long hiatus as a prestige shoe, until the addition of high heels in the 1920s made them newly glamorous.

S H O E S

are the first adult machines

we are given to master.

NICHOLSON BAKER

MULE Backlessness defines the 4,500-year-old mule, the ancestor of slides. Its name comes from the Sumerian word *mulu* ("indoor shoe"). The first mules were flat; the Egyptians added low heels so they could be worn outdoors. A 17th-century French adaptation called the *mulette* added a higher, more coquettish heel. Decked out with high heels and ostrich feathers, like those Marilyn Monroe wore in *The Seven Year Itch,* mules can be one of the most erotic shoes imaginable. Of course, when not worn by Monroe, they can be tacky.

BOOT Mongolian horsemen wore boots (footwear extending above the ankle) around 600 BCE. But in Europe, boots began about a thousand years ago as shoes with leggings attached, which later became single pieces of footwear. The French cavaliers favored a thigh-high, flare-topped *butt* ("water bucket"), a style that pirates and smugglers also found convenient for stashing contraband, hence the word *bootleg.* In 1066, the Normans brought the *butt* to England, where it became the boot. By 1800, boots had become stylish for both men and women. Their aura of aggressiveness links them to sex, the rubber mucking-about boot notwithstanding.

MONK OR CLOG A slip-on with a wide strap across the in-step, the monk is thought to have originated around 1400 in a monastery in the Alps. Buckles, invented in the 1600s, were added later to anchor the strap. The monk is related to the ancient clog,

Achilles' Heel

Achilles, the hero of Homer's epic poem the *Iliad,* is killed by an arrow to the heel, the only part of his body vulnerable to fatal injury. This because his mother, the sea goddess Thetis, married a mortal (an occupational hazard for Greek gods, always interfering in the affairs of the unruly humans). When Achilles was a baby, Thetis tried to give him immortality by dipping him in the river Styx. Unfortunately, she held him by the heel, keeping it out of the water rather than get her hand wet, which makes you wonder what she was thinking. Years later, Paris launches the fatal shot, fulfilling Achilles' destiny, as well as providing a name for the vulnerable tendon joining heel to calf and for the dramatic device familiar in art as in life, the tragic mortal weakness.

which peasants first made by carving an opening in a block of wood. European clogs, called sabots, became handy weapons of sabotage during the Industrial Revolution of the 1800s, when angry workers hurled them into the machinery.

PUMP The pump began in 16th-century Britain as a simple low-cut slipper, something like a ballet flat, which was held on with a wraparound strap. The first high-ish heels were very unstable. It wasn't until the turn of the 20th century that technology was available to construct the stiff but still flexible soles required to support a really high heel. Women's pumps or "court" shoes eventually came to mean high-heeled slippers. The name may refer to 19th-century pump men, who wore similar shoes to pump the hydraulic systems of carriages. ➤

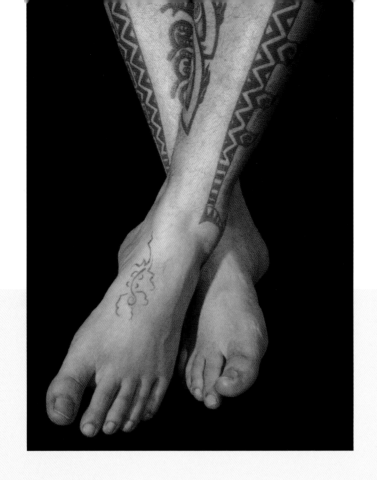

That **I AM** *part of the earth*

MY FEET *know perfectly.*

D.H. LAWRENCE

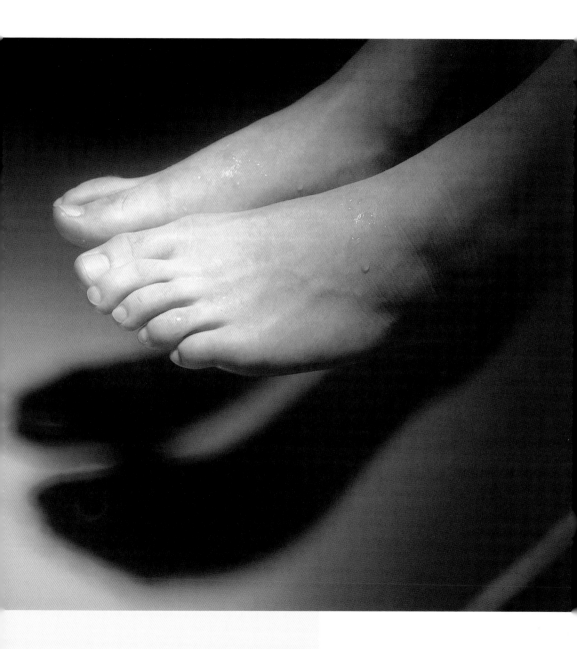

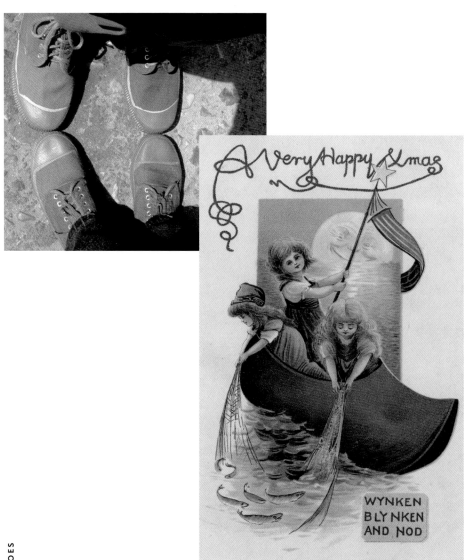

Very Happy Xmas

WYNKEN
BLYNKEN
AND NOD

ARTCRAFT
*Stockings
of Elegance*

I still have my feet on the ground,
I just wear better shoes.

OPRAH WINFREY

OXFORD The oxford, the shoe type invented most recently, originated in 1640 in Oxford, England, where university students snapped it up. The first oxfords were simple low-cut shoe-boots tied with laces. Eventually the shoe had the characteristic vamp (toe covering) stitched to the quarters (side and back pieces), which met and laced up in front. This sturdy, no-nonsense shoe is thought to be have been inspired by laced corsets, which shows how minds can drift.

Wedding Feet

. . . .

BECAUSE THEY TOUCH the earth, feet have long been thought prey to evil spirits. Nothing could be less welcome at a wedding, so people have invented dozens of ways to keep them at bay.

The Berbers of Morocco decorate brides' feet and shoes with intricate henna designs. After the ceremony, the new wife often rides a donkey to the groom's home to keep her feet safely off the ground.

Shoes are considered lucky at weddings, perhaps because they enclose the feet or symbolize sexual union. Tying shoes to or throwing them at the wedding vehicle may have begun in Tudor England and was *de rigueur* at weddings a century ago. Emily Post informed brides in the 1920s that the "greatest good fortune" would accrue to a couple if a tossed white slipper landed right-side up on top of the wedding car and stayed there.

Throwing shoes at the couple themselves is one of the most popular of all wedding customs. The practice is thought to symbolize the battle between the bride's and the groom's tribesmen as he steals her away. It could also, less romantically, relate to property transfer—the Assyrians, Hebrews, and Egyptians all gave or exchanged shoes as part of property-sale transactions.

In an old Saxon tradition that persisted through the Middle Ages, the bride's father presented the groom with one of the girl's shoes, symbolizing his transfer of authority. The groom would immediately alert the bride to this new state of affairs by tapping her on the head with it. (In return, he promised to treat her well, never mind the head-tapping incident.)

In Sweden in the 19th century, the bride's parents gave her lucky coins to put in her shoe. A Scottish bride would have her feet bathed by friends and would then tuck a silver coin into her left shoe. A Macedonian groom gave his bride a new pair of shoes, which guests needed to stuff with many gold coins before they "fit" properly.

REALLY FAST FOOD

In November 2000, American Rob Williams whipped up a bologna, cheese, and salad sandwich, using only his feet, in 1 minute, 57 seconds, setting a world record.

During Javanese wedding ceremonies, the groom breaks an egg with his foot, signifying his intention to be a good provider and his hope for children. The bride shows her devotion by washing his foot in water sprinkled with rose and jasmine petals. The Jewish groom breaks a wine glass under his foot, symbolizing the destruction of the temple of Jerusalem. It's not too much of a stretch to suppose that breakage may also symbolize the consummation of the marriage.

Forensic Feet

. . . .

*I*F THE SHOE FITS ... it may belong to a killer, thief, or missing person. In the world of criminal investigation, shoes, socks, and feet can provide important clues.

Bare feet leave footprints—traces of oil and perspiration from the skin. The prints can be dusted, photographed, and lifted with tape. Prints left in blood can be dusted with a hardening substance. Photographs or casts can be taken of three-dimensional prints left in soft surfaces like mud, sand, or even snow.

The investigator, who might be a forensic anthropologist or podiatrist, looks for something distinctive. Barefoot prints might show physical features such as calluses or clawing of the toes; shoe prints might show wear patterns indicating biomechanical characteristics of the owner's walk, such as overpronation (rolling in). These records can then be compared to suspects' feet, shoes, or gait patterns.

Unlike fingerprints, however, footprints can only suggest, not prove identification. With footprints, there are no hard scientific facts to provide positive matching. They don't show the individually unique loops and whorls that have made fingerprints so valuable as forensic evidence, nor is there an immense data bank of prints to check against. Still, the temptation to overstate or even falsify evidence can sometimes be irresistible. In one notorious case in the 1990s, an American anthropology professor made a name for herself by claiming that she could identify anyone by his or her footprints. For a decade she served as an expert witness in murder trials all over North America. Her testimony sent a dozen people to jail and put one on death row before her "science" was shown to be faulty.

YOU CANNOT PUT THE *same shoe* ON EVERY FOOT.

PUBLIUS SYRUS, 42 BCE

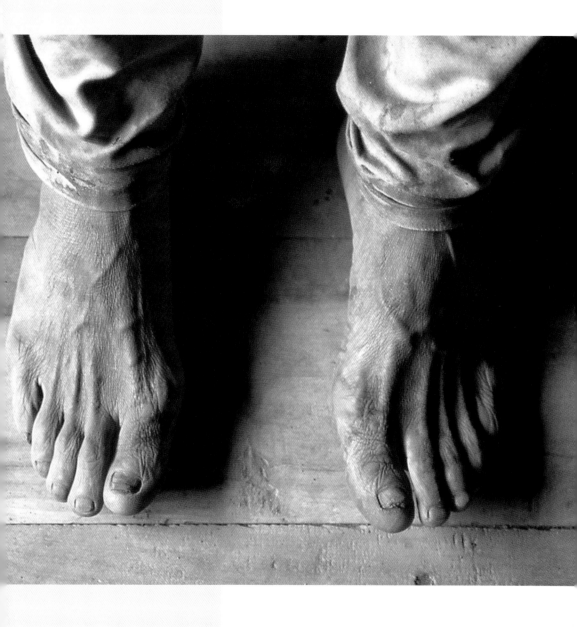

DAY OF THE

*F*EW DETAILS OF FOOT lore perplex modern
minds more than the ancient Chinese custom of footbinding. At
its worst, the process was brutal. It began when a girl was about
six. After a ritual of prayers and offerings, the footbinder (often the
mother) would soak the child's feet in hot water and massage them
with medicinal powders. Then she wound a long, narrow cloth
tightly around each foot in a figure-eight pattern, bending the four

STAND [STAND] *VB.*

· · · · · ·

RISE TO OR MAINTAIN

· · · · · ·

AN ERECT POSITION

· · · · · ·

ON THE FEET.

LOTUS

smaller toes underneath, bowing the arch, and bringing the heel

and forefoot close together. The bindings were sewn shut and a

pair of small shoes forced on. Finally, the child was made to stand

and walk to prevent her traumatized feet from quickly dying.

For two years, the bindings would be regularly tightened and

progressively smaller shoes wrenched on. Often the child's feet

reeked of pus and blood. Flesh rotted and fell away, and sometimes toes dropped off. Some girls died. The terrible pain lasted a year or two before subsiding. But if the gods smiled, the girl's reward would be a pair of "golden lotuses"—each foot an incredible three-inch-long appendage tapering from rounded heel to pointed big toe, with a high, bowed arch and a narrow cleft separating heel and forefoot. Her natural feet would have become idealized fantasy creations.

Next came the girl's hand-sewn wardrobe of exquisitely embroidered lotus slippers, much coveted by admirers as fetishes. The toe-tips would be glimpsed peeking out enticingly beneath yards of leggings and skirts or, by a lucky lover, reclining on silk sheets. (Many women wore special red slippers even to bed.)

The final element was the girl's peculiar walk. Taking mincing steps, she undulated in a manner that men found intoxicating. The total effect was a mix of grace, dependency, discipline, and implied sexuality, which defined femininity in Han culture.

This intricate scenario was a powerful aphrodisiac for men. A whole body of Chinese erotica details the raptures of sex with bound-footed courtesans. Connoisseurs found it deeply arousing to hold the tiny feet in their hands, sip wine from a dainty slipper, nibble on the foot, or rub the cleft in the arch.

At least, this is the story that Westerners have come to know. But according to historians such as Dorothy Ko, a professor at Columbia University, it's a distorted view, based on accounts written since the 19th century. Much older documents suggest that footbinding was a more complex and interesting practice altogether, its details varying according to time and place. For instance, footbinding could refer to different kinds of loose binding (popular with male actors) or even tight-fitting socks. Some women didn't bind at all.

Its cultural meaning varied too and was often contradictory. In the 10th century, binding was confined to women of the court as a sign of prestige. By its heyday in the Ming dynasty (1368–1644), it had spread throughout the upper classes and had become part of the very definition of Han culture and morality. By the late 17th century, women of every class were binding their feet. No longer a status symbol, footbinding had become both completely conventional (at home) and rather lewd (in the brothels). ➤

BOUND *feet,*

bound FEET,

PAST THE *gate*

can't RETREAT.

CHINESE RHYME, 1900

An important part of the picture—how women perceived footbinding—is largely missing from the records, since men wrote most of them. But it's clear that in some ways, women used it to their own advantage. A pair of golden lotuses did provide a rare means of social mobility, allowing women of lower rank to marry up. More provocatively, women's literature from the 17th century suggests that the bound foot was a focus of romantic and homoerotic life in the inner chambers.

The Ritual Foot

FOOTWEAR ALFRESCO In many parts of Asia and the Middle East, guests remove their shoes when entering a house. Shoes in this case represent the polluted "outside"; leaving them at the door respects the physical and spiritual cleanliness of the home and acknowledges the honor of being invited into a private space.

FOOTBATH Before motorized travel, people walked almost everywhere they needed to go, often in sandals. By the time they arrived at someone's home, their feet were grimy, so it wasn't enough to take off their shoes. They would wash their feet, or in a wealthy home, have them washed by the servants. Water is an

Pardon My Feet

The essential rudeness of feet and legs has been long acknowledged. In *The Rituals of Dinner*, Margaret Visser quotes the English writer John Russell as exhorting 15th-century guests not to "trample with your feet, or straddle your legs; jetting is bad manners." Apparently, "jetting"—bouncing the legs up and down or thrusting them in and out—was a habit popular enough to warrant special sanction. In homes in the Middle East and parts of Asia today, guests are careful to keep their feet to themselves. Making a show of your feet or legs, especially when food is being served, is considered offensive, feet being both polluting and very intimate parts of the body.

ancient purification symbol, so the practice worked on several levels. Probably the best-known example of the old custom is the biblical story of Christ washing his disciples' feet at the Last Supper (John 13:1–17). Jesus assures the dismayed disciples that someday they will understand the symbolic meaning of his act, which Christian scholars interpret as a lesson in service and humility, two fundamental Christian virtues.

Foot washing survives in many places today as a gesture of respect. In Nepal, an old custom asks wives to show their devotion by washing their husbands' feet. However, wives no longer feel obliged to drink the water afterwards.

HEART AND SOLE An ancient Greek might carve his lover's name on the bottom of his sandals to leave its sweet imprint in the dust wherever he walked. In a harsher application of that logic,

Think of the magic of that foot,

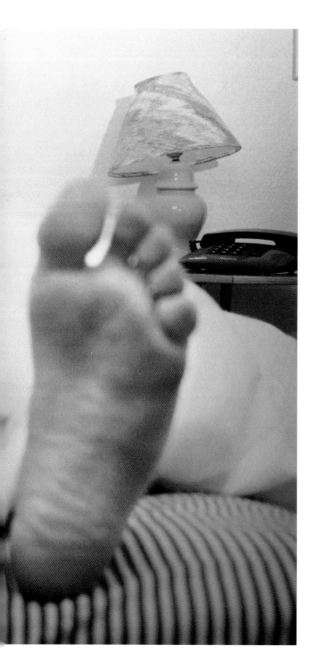

comparatively small,

upon which your

whole weight rests.

MARTHA GRAHAM

Egyptians and Romans inscribed the names or pictures of their enemies on their soles so they could crush them with every step.

PUCKER UP AND... Kissing the feet of a person of high rank acknowledges the authority or holiness of the kissee and the humility and devotion of the kisser. The Greeks and Romans paid homage to their gods and later monarchs in the practice of kissing one's own hand and waving it in the direction of the adored one, a custom that sometimes extended to kissing the monarch's feet. In the Roman Church, kissing the pope's feet may go back to the emperor Diocletian, whose gesture was adopted by the popes. Homage is often paid to images of the exalted. So many pilgrims have bussed the feet of the Statue of Saint Peter in Rome that they've gotten a bit worn down.

SPIRIT CHASERS Homeowners in Europe have sometimes been startled to find ancient shoes tucked away in the rafters, floorboards, or chimneys. In England, hiding shoes for luck goes back at least to the 14th century, when John Schorn, rector of North Marston, Buckinghamshire, is said to have cast the devil into a boot. Until the industrial age, shoes were very expensive personal items, so by the time a shoe was ready to be tossed, it bore the foot imprint and other remnants of the life of its owner. This may have made it useful as a decoy for evil spirits, similar to a witch-bottle. The spirits would be fooled into thinking the owner was in the shoe and would get trapped there, unable to wreak havoc on the real person. Sometimes a whole family of shoes would be cached together, built into the house as it was going up.

FOOTBURN

"Trial by fire" was once more than a metaphor. In Europe during the Middle Ages and until recently in parts of Africa and Asia, the fiery ordeal was a common legal means of deciding the fate of accused parties. One form was to have the wretch walk through fire or over hot plowshares. The belief was that if the person was innocent, God would protect him or her.

FRIEND, FOE, OR FOOT Traditionally, the Scots' celebration of Hogmanay includes an element of high drama when the clock strikes midnight New Year's Eve. The first person to set foot in your home determines the family's fortune for the rest of the year. Everyone hopes for a tall, dark stranger bearing gifts of a cake, a coin, or coal for the fire. (At least let him not be blond, a dread that might trace back to the Vikings and their reputed bad habit of raping and pillaging.) In return, you give the guest food and a wee dram. Today, what's more likely to turn up at the door after midnight on January 1 is a group of partygoers, at least one of whom is sure to be dark.

And GET *a comfortable* WIFE

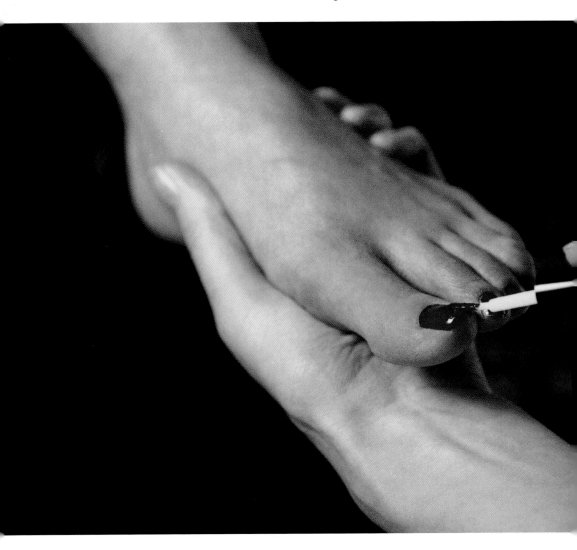

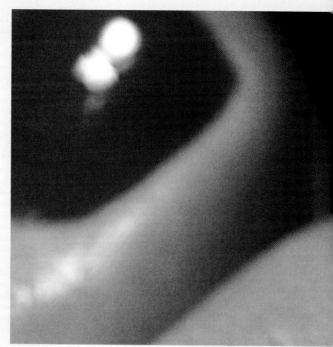

and **HOUSE**

To **RID** *me of the devil*

in my **SHOES**

W.B. YEATS

Phenomenal Feet

. . . .

*S*TIGMATA—PAINFUL WOUNDS imitating those of the crucified Christ that appear spontaneously on the feet, hands, and sides of susceptible people—have baffled doctors since St. Francis of Assisi broke out with the first case in 1224. Shaped like nails protruding from the sides of his hands and feet (heads on one side, points on the other), his stigmata were a hard act to follow, but the Catholic Church has since documented hundreds of less baroque cases of what the afflicted claim to be divine manifestations.

Most stigmatics have been women and Catholics (often nuns) from Mediterranean or Latin countries, though the profile has expanded considerably since the 20th century. Some recent cases have had quite earthly beginnings. Father James Bruce, an American priest who claimed the stigmata in the early 1990s, had in his early days gotten himself into the *Guinness Book of World Records* for longest roller-coaster ride (five straight days).

Stigmata tend to be various kinds of flesh wounds, sometimes bleeding and often appearing and disappearing at regular intervals. A 16th-century Italian nun, St. Catherine de' Ricci, for instance, received the stigmata every Thursday noon until Friday at 4 p.m. A striking feature of stigmata is their extreme variety, which can include claimed psychic abilities such as clairvoyance or levitation. For many observers, this proves they are inauthentic, at least as spiritual visitations.

Not that it's known for sure how Christ's wounds looked—the Romans used many methods of crucifixion. The skeletal remains of only one 1st-century victim have been found so far. Discovered in Jerusalem in 1968, they belong to a man named Jehohanan, whose calcaneus (heel bone) has a nail driven through its side, indicating that he was crucified with his legs bent sideways. What stigmata seem to reflect is the sufferer's own image of the crucifixion, which often matches a personal reference such as a statue in the local church.

Leaving aside a miraculous explanation, stigmata appear to be either fakes or psychosomatic phenomena. Faking (sometimes for pious reasons) is common and, in fact, despite repeated attempts, it is possible that no outside observer has ever seen the onset or bleeding of any stigmatic wounds. In the 1950s, a doctor keeping the Bavarian stigmatic Therese Neumann under surveillance reported that her bleeding started only when he was out of the room or after periods of suspicious maneuvering under tented bed sheets. ➤

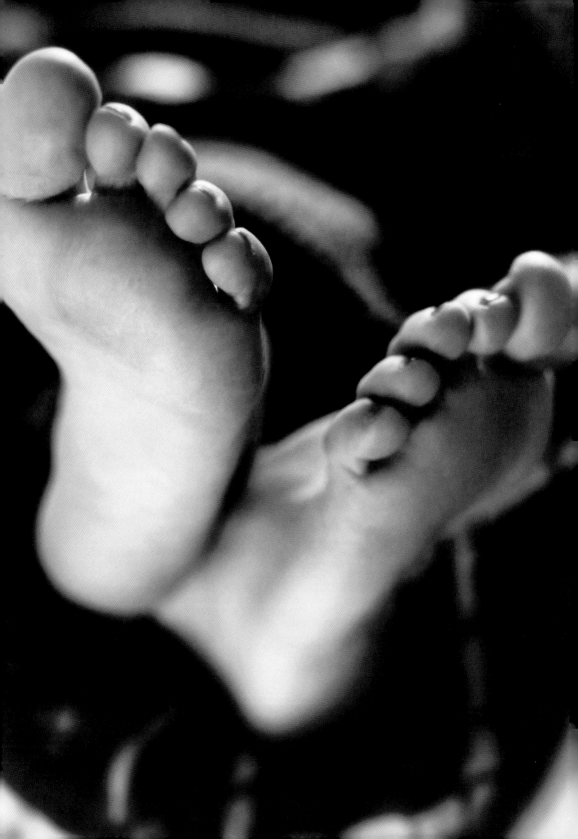

I LIKE *the* WAY
MY **OWN** FEET SMELL.
I *love* TO SMELL
MY **SNEAKERS** WHEN I
TAKE THEM *off*.

CHRISTINA RICCI

The second possibility is more interesting. Some doctors think stigmata may be psychogenic purpuras, areas of spontaneous bleeding into the skin, of unknown organic origin. Perhaps the more spectacular effects are not so much unexplainable as yet to be explained.

Walking Through Fire

. . . .

*H*UMANS SEEM irresistibly drawn to the idea of walking barefoot over hot coals. Firewalking, an ancient purification rite common to many cultures, is still practiced today in such far-flung parts of the world as the Fiji Islands, Trinidad, Mauritius, Bulgaria, and Japan. Near Tokyo, for instance, an annual spring festival mixing Buddhist and Shinto elements attracts large crowds of mystics and lay visitors to the firewalking ceremony, many of whom eagerly join in.

The ritual is also quite popular in North America and Europe, where things play out a little differently. Tapping into several current trends, promoters of firewalking advertise it as a health benefit, leadership-training technique, or means to spiritual growth. Thousands of people have tried it (one U.S. company claims to have shepherded more than 2 million customers safely over the coals), and many report its powerful, life-changing effects.

What's it like? Virginia Schwartz, a New York writer, remembers the night she and some friends, all feeling in need of a psychic jolt, walked over a 20-foot-long bed of hot coals.

"We had been told to meditate," she recalls, "and if we felt pain to immediately draw our minds away from the physical to the spiritual—not to think, not to be 'in the body.'

"I almost glided. I knew I was walking over coals and that the heat while standing there had been so intense on that spring night that I had taken off my jacket. But actually walking on the coals, I felt nothing. I went over them like it was just a sidewalk. When I was done, I felt as if I was soaring up to heaven. I laughed so hard, and then I cried. It felt freeing and releasing, and I twirled like a kid around and around in circles. When I examined my feet, there was no mark." ➤

Size Matters

The Guinness world record (2002) for largest feet belongs to a Florida man who is 7 feet 4 inches tall, weighs 617 pounds, and wears size 28 1/2 shoes, which cost him up to $22,745 a pair. A grandmother in California has the longest toenails, each measuring about 6 inches long and probably requiring quite large shoes as well. A Sri Lankan, Arulananthan Suresh Joachim, balanced the longest on one foot (76 hours, 40 minutes) in May 1997. And Argentinian Claudia Gomez holds the record (as of November 2001) for farthest foot-archery shot, at 18 feet 4 inches. Foot archery—in which archers, from a handstand, shoot an arrow into a target with their feet—requires acrobatic as well as athletic skill and is sometimes performed as a circus act.

ENGLISHWOMEN'S **SHOES**

look as if they

HAD BEEN MADE BY

someone

WHO HAD **OFTEN** HEARD

shoes described

BUT HAD **NEVER**

seen any.

MARGARET HALSEY,
WITH MALICE TOWARD SOME

Skeptics argue that anyone can walk over smoldering coals without pain or injury, that the coals are wood, a relatively poor conductor of heat, and that in a typical walk of about five yards, each foot is in contact with the fire for only a second or two. Organizers make the walks safe, they say, by lighting the fire several hours in advance, using woods that don't ooze sap that can stick to the toes, raking plenty of ash over the firebed, advising people to walk briskly, and keeping the walks short.

But proponents of the walks say that the key protective element is an altered consciousness, a kind of self-hypnosis that controls physical experience. "What stayed with me," Schwartz says, "was that I'd had an experience of eternity, of slipping through time. I'm glad I tried it rather than turning away. It was the start of many risks I took to push myself out of myself."

Rhodopis' Slipper

POSSIBLY THE EARLIEST of all Cinderella tales comes from ancient Egypt. This version is stripped down and win–win. One day, the beauteous and tiny-footed Rhodopis is bathing by the River Nile when an eagle swoops down and takes off with one of her slippers. The bird deposits it at the feet of the pharaoh, who is so enraptured by it that he searches the kingdom to find the owner and marry her. The king tries the shoe on scores of maidenly feet, eventually finds Rhodopis, and makes her his queen. He then builds a pyramid in her honor.

The heroine of this legend may be modeled after a real Rhodopis mentioned by the Greek historian Herodotus. His Rhodopis lives in Egypt in the 4th century BCE. She grows up as a Greek slave in the same household as the fabulist Aesop, then gets sold and taken to Egypt, where her beauty catches the eye of Charaxos, a Greek merchant and brother of the renowned poet Sappho. (Rhodopis seems not only bodacious but very well connected.) Charaxos buys the girl's freedom, and she becomes a rich courtesan whose fame spreads throughout Egypt and Greece. Herodotus has nothing to say about her feet.

I could see *very clearly* the thick pads of **hardened** skin

on the **soles** of his feet. They were *dirty* and

cracked and there were little strips **peeling** off the side. As a courtier

my **father** had *never* been allowed to wear shoes.

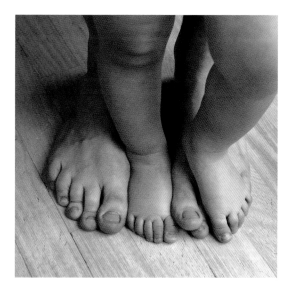

B U T

he had bought

S H O E S

for me.

V.S. NAIPAUL, HALF A LIFE

W BAD

ITH PROPER TREATMENT and a little luck, a
pair of feet should last a lifetime without pain or disease. But that
rarely happens—sometimes good feet go bad.

BUNIONS A bunion is a bony swelling at the first joint of
the big toe, where body weight falls with every step. Typically the
big toe bends inward and may overlap its neighbors. The
deformity can be severe, making walking extremely painful.

RUN [RUN] *VB.*

· · · · · ·

MOVE SWIFTLY AND

· · · · · ·

FREELY ON FOOT

DOGS

Bunions may be associated with a hereditary weakness in foot

structure, arthritis, age, or years of wearing tight, pointed shoes

that squeeze the toes.

HEEL SPUR This bony knob sprouts from the bottom of

the heel bone and presses on nerves and tissues as you walk or

stand. Heel spurs are a response to excessive strain on the muscles,

tendons, and ligaments of the heel and sole by running or jogging

BEYOND BUNIONS

. . . .

Feet have joined crow's feet as
targets for surgical enhancement.
Well-heeled but sadly soled fashion-
istas can have their toes made longer
or shorter, or the balls of their feet
plumped up with collagen, a boon
for shopping in stilettos.

too much, walking incorrectly, wearing the wrong shoes, or being overweight.

ATHLETE'S FOOT The name may take some of the sting out of what is in fact a lowly fungus infection that anyone can get. Anyone who wears shoes, that is. By enclosing your feet, you create a nice moist, warm, airless environment where the fungi thrive on the keratin (a protein) in your skin.

RAYNAUD'S SYNDROME This startling condition strikes women four times as often as men and may be brought on by stress. Raynaud's is a circulatory disorder in which nerves in the blood vessels of the extremities cause arteries to clamp shut spasmodically at the slightest drop in temperature—standing in front of an open refrigerator, for instance. Toes or fingers may suddenly turn white, then blue, then red, usually over a few minutes. The condition is usually not serious but can stop conversation in a room.

GOUT Gout was once considered a disease of decadence, its typical sufferer a corpulent old male aristocrat devoted to the pleasures of brandy and fatty food. Excruciatingly painful attacks would strike the big toe joint, which became inflamed and swollen. In fact, the disease does disproportionately target overweight men, but they don't have to be rich, old, or any more decadent than the next fellow. Gout occurs when the body can't get rid of excess uric acid in the blood, causing crystals of sodium urate to form around the joints of the big toe (and sometimes other joints). Gout is a form of arthritis and may be associated with injury, stress, alcohol, rich food, or certain drugs.

CLUBFEET Clubfoot is known medically as *talipes equinovarus,* a descriptive term for a congenital condition in which the foot is turned down and inward. (*Equus,* Latin for "horse," refers to the foot's down-turning position.) Most infants with clubfeet are otherwise entirely healthy. Clubfeet have been with us since at least a thousand years BCE. Even the gods of Olympus were not immune: Vulcan, god of fire, had a clubfoot, the only physical deformity ➤

Walkabout

The human body has been fine-tuned over millions of years for walking upright. We can balance on two pins because of a complex synchronization of the visual and inner ear systems, and nerve signals in the muscles and joints. Our leg bones and muscles are long and much stronger than our arms, capable of carrying more than two and a half times our body weight when running. Our spines are curved and our pelvic bones tipped and bowl-shaped for flexibility and strength. Our feet are arched levers with forward-pointing big toes, built to function most efficiently for two-legged locomotion.

The

DOCTOR

remarked on the

EXTREME LIVENESS

of my feet nerves.

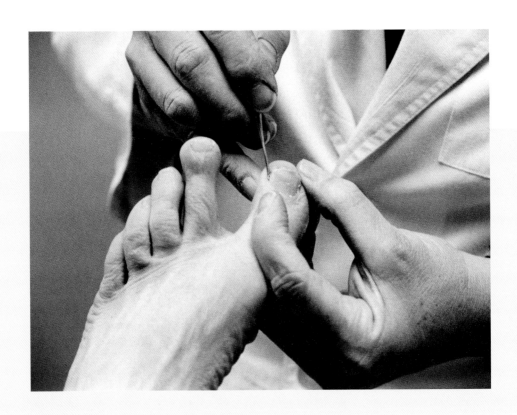

Underfoot *things can do things*
to my whole being—
exquisite pain and **exquisite** *pleasure.*
There you are.

EMILY CARR, HUNDREDS AND THOUSANDS

borne by a Greco-Roman deity. The poet Byron had one too, and like Vulcan was rejected for it by women he desired, until his genius made him famous.

For many people, clubfoot is indelibly associated with a horror story from literature. In Flaubert's *Madame Bovary,* the good doctor Bovary, attempting to impress his chronically dissatisfied wife, tries to fix the clubfoot of the stable-boy Hippolyte using an experimental surgical procedure he's learned from a book. Gangrene sets in and the poor boy's leg must be amputated. Fortunately, that's a worst-case scenario unlikely to happen today in real life.

About one in a thousand babies is born with the disorder, whose cause is not always known. With treatment, most children have normal-looking and functioning feet by walking age.

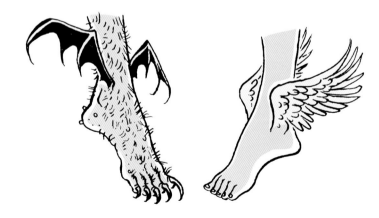

Walkways

Humans and a few other animals, such as bears, are plantigrades, meaning they walk on the entire sole of the foot. In digitigrade animals, such as tigers and wolves, the weight falls on a pad behind the toes, while the ankle and wrist are held up in the air.

Unguligrades, such as horses and goats, walk on hard, nail-like structures (hooves) at the end of one or more toes. Because we like to have it all ways, humans effect a more digitigrade stance with high heels, while many enjoy the unguligrade feel of platforms.

Barefooting It

MOST PEOPLE LOVE to go barefoot when they can, but they assume they need footgear for safety, convenience, propriety, and—well, to look good.

Others would say wrong on all counts. The U.S.–based Society for Barefoot Living, for instance, claims close to a thousand members in 45 countries, all eager to strip off their sandals and free their soles—everywhere, all the time. This band of shoeless nonconformists regularly brave not only the physical trials of city streets and hiking trails, even in cold weather, but also the censure of restaurant owners, school officials, and their neighbors. The payoff, they claim, is healthier feet and the joy of a natural, vibrantly sensuous experience. ➤

The

FOOT

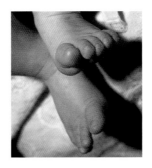

IS A SYMBOL OF

the soul.

J.E. CIRLOT,

A DICTIONARY OF SYMBOLS

Research tends to back them up. Podiatrists report that only 4 percent of barefooters experience foot problems compared to 70 percent of shoe wearers. Millions of shoe-free people in developing cultures navigate forests and savannahs without difficulty, and their feet are generally stronger, more flexible, and freer from deformity and disease than those of the shoddies.

No shoe eschewer suggests going barefoot in sub-zero temperatures or at a construction site. But walking—even hiking—in moderate climes can be done safely and comfortably. (The trick is to watch where you're going and step straight down.) Freed feet, barefooters claim, soon relearn their natural role as sensory feelers and begin again to respond to the myriad textures of the natural world.

Devotees believe that going barefoot is also relaxing, and kind to the environment, and looks fine—especially with a few toe rings and anklets. The greatest challenge for barefooters is finding social acceptability in a world wedded to footwear. They're puzzled, they say, by the taboo against feet. This is the real motive behind the "No shirt, no shoes, no service" signs in restaurant windows. Legally and rationally speaking, there is nothing objectionable about bare feet. It's the ancient and still-potent taboos that ultimately stand between barefooters and their dreams.

Sole Healing

. . . .

*P*RACTITIONERS OF REFLEXOLOGY believe they can alleviate many symptoms by massaging specific zones on the feet or hands that correspond to various body parts or systems. The base of the big toe, for instance, corresponds to the neck and throat. According to this ancient system (Cleopatra is said to have worked on Marc Antony's feet), stimulating these zones breaks down energy blocks that are the cause of disease or pain. The goal is to activate the body's self-healing process and bring the body into balance.

RIGHT, LEFT

. . . .

It wasn't until the 19th century that technology was available to easily craft mirror-image shoes for right and left feet. Before then, most shoes were "straights."

The Soulful Foot

. . . .

*S*EXY, INNOCENT, BEAUTIFUL, prosaic, sensuous, strong, vulnerable—feet are all those and more. They've also got soul.

Many ancient traditions consider the foot sacred. In Greek mythology, the foot represented the state and destiny of the soul. A wound to the foot of a hero such as Achilles thus signified a disconnection between humanity and the universe. (Although the über-god Zeus himself suffered a foot injury, suggesting that perfect alignment with the heavens may not be possible.)

Buddhists kiss the feet of Buddha images. Christians express their symbolic meaning in rituals of foot washing. Yoga also recognizes the spiritual nature of the foot, which connects the body to the earth and its gravitational force. Devotees are conscious of being rooted to the ground like trees, freeing their spines to expand upward. The flow of energy from the heels to the top of the head reflects the link between earth and sky, the human and the divine.

Clearly, feet are treasures to be cared for, respected, cherished, and even adored.

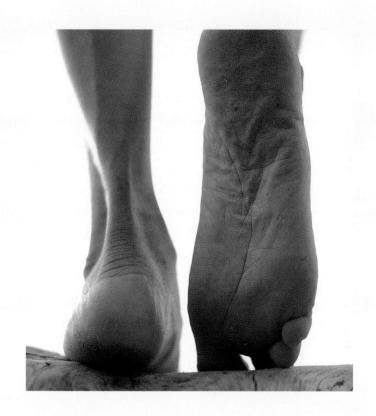

The foot feels the foot

WHEN IT FEELS THE GROUND.

BUDDHA

Acknowledgements

. . . .

*M*ANY THANKS to the following for helping me get my feet off the ground: Elizabeth Semmelhack, curator, Suzanne McLean, and Ainsley Cameron of the Bata Shoe Museum, Toronto; Dr. Kathy Gruspier; Margo Huc; Dan Jost; Kevin and Cole Kowalchuk; Doreen Makepeace; Dr. Susan Pfeiffer; Paul and Sami Davis Safarian; Virginia Schwartz; Nicole Stoffman; Simon Tanenbaum; Dr. Loren Vanderlinden; Dr. Myriam Zylstra; members of the Editors' Association of Canada e-list; the staff at Camden Spa: and Jay at Passage Tattoos & Body Piercing. Special thanks to the Greystone gang, Rob Sanders, Nancy Flight, Mary Schendlinger, Susan Rana, Peter Cocking, Jessica Sullivan, and Roxanna Bikadoroff, for their boundless talent, faith, and enthusiasm. Extra special thanks to Tony Makepeace.

Illustration credits

. . . .